My Good Mood Book

Contents

Written by Rachael Davis

Illustrated by Claudio Cerri

Collins

Feelings and mood

Feelings can impact the mood we are in.
A feeling can be fleeting and quick
to go. A mood hangs on for longer.

Can you explain
what the children
here are feeling?

cross

glad

afraid

shocked

disappointed

Keeping track of feelings

Tracking good things can limit feelings of sadness, disappointment and gloom.

Start tracking things you feel good
seeing or doing.

Spotting good things

Start training! Spot good things and point them out.

Can you spot the good things that are happening here?

Did you spot them all?

You can train the brain to look for good things. This can help spark a good mood.

How to keep a feel-good mood book

Think of three good things from today. Jot them down in the book.

Did you feel good when ...

... you had
a hug?

... you looked
at the stars
at night?

... you sat
under the trees?

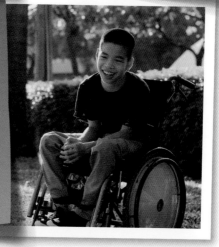

Keeping track of good things can spark a good mood and help you feel contentment for longer.

Looking back can help you to feel glad.

Keep a feel-good mood book

spot it

jot it down

feel glad

🐾 Review: After reading 🐾

Use your assessment from hearing the children read to choose any GPCs, words or tricky words that need additional practice.

Read 1: Decoding

- Turn to page 12 and point to the word **spark**. Ask the children to read pages 12 and 13, and then explain the meaning of "spark". (e.g. *create, bring about, inspire*)

- Encourage the children to practise reading words with adjacent consonants. Suggest that they sound out longer words in syllables or chunks.

  glad   cross   from   gloom   train/ing   con/tent/ment   dis/app/oint/ment

- On pages 6 and 7, point to the following words for the children to read aloud. Challenge them to blend the words silently in their heads.

  start   spot   point   happening

Read 2: Prosody

- Ask the children to look out for the commas, ellipses and question marks as you model reading pages 10 and 11.

- Discuss how you paused for commas and the ellipses, and emphasised the exclamatory **thank you!** on page 10. Did they notice how your tone went up at the end of the questions?

- Encourage the children to read pages 10 and 11, pausing and changing their tone appropriately.

Read 3: Comprehension

- Read the question on the back cover blurb together, and ask the children to describe times they have felt good, and why.

- Discuss whether this statement is true: "This book tells us how to do something." (e.g. *it tells us how to feel good; it tells us how to make a feel-good mood book*)

- Turn to pages 14 and 15, and discuss the order of the three stages of instructions. Ask:

  o How can we find examples of good things to spot? (*Look back at the Contents or refer back to page 11.*)

  o How many things should we start tracking? (*three, page 10*)

  o What might happen as we jot down the good things? (*it might spark a good mood, page 12*)

  o Invite the children to use pages 14 and 15 to help them plan an entry for their own good mood book.